To

That's Not Happening

A strong & loving
woman whom I.
cherish and admire

enjoy

w/ love

Karen

Aug 20, 2016.

That's Not Happening

HOW TO FIND HUMOUR AND STRENGTH IN A MISDIAGNOSIS

Karen Davidson Zachary

ISBN: 0995095205
ISBN 13: 9780995095205

To Sandra,
who taught me that grace under pressure is
beautiful, dignity can be rewarding, and humility
is the best gift we can give ourselves. Thank
you for being my friend and for being in my life.

"Well-behaved women rarely make history."

—LAUREL THATCHER ULRICH

Table of Contents

Prologue

I WROTE THIS BOOK BECAUSE what happened to me shouldn't have happened.

I want people to realize that you have options when it comes to your health and your life, that when you are backed into a corner, you shouldn't cower. You should come out with a sword and slay whatever dragon is in your way.

This is your life, so *you* get to make the choices and *you* get to decide how you are going to handle those choices. I believe it is important to move ahead, knowing you are always going to survive.

My dear friend thinks we have expiry dates on our asses, and when it's time to go, we get scanned, and that's it. None of us knows what our life expectancy is, but every day is a clean slate, no mistakes.

So get up, give it your best, and don't take crap from anyone.

Cast of Characters

Dr. Sangfroid	~	Local Hematologist
Nurse Merry	~	Local Cancer Unit Nurse
Dr. Kevin	~	Local General Practitioner
Dr. Gentil	~	Local Neurologist
Dr. DeVain	~	Ottawa Hospital Oncologist
Dr. Lamb	~	Ottawa Hospital Hematologist
Dr. Doom	~	Ottawa Hospital Hematologist
Dr. Power	~	Ottawa Hospital Neurologist
Dr. Gray	~	Ottawa Hospital Hematologist
Dr. Sage	~	Ottawa Hospital Chief Hematologist
Liz	~	Counsellor

| Katie | ~ | Coordinator, Bone Marrow Unit, Ottawa |
| Henry Houdini | ~ | Ottawa Hospital Pharmacist |

*The characters listed above are fictitious. Any similarity to real persons, living or dead, is coincidental and not intended by the author.

**I am grateful to have permission to use the real names of family and friends.

CHAPTER 1

Only the Good Die Young

"You have a year to a year and a half," Dr. Sangfroid said to me dryly, like he was the toll taker on my life and he had just given me my balance.

As he continued to talk, my brain shut down and it felt like I was in a car on black ice, careening all over the place.

Absurd questions were bouncing around inside my head: *How'd he get that fucking phone off his belt so fast when I asked that question? That can't be why doctors keep them on their belts, is it? Just to tell people when they're going to die? Did he have my prognosis bookmarked when he walked in here?*

Dirty Harry couldn't have taken his gun off his belt any faster. But the last thing I remember thinking before I pulled myself together was, *A year to a year and a half? THAT'S NOT FUCKING HAPPENING! It can't. I have things to do and dying isn't one of them.*

At this point, my imaginary car ride came to a screeching halt, as if it had hit a telephone pole, and I came back to my senses. I glanced at my husband, Bob. He looked like he had been in the car with me and now understood that everything I had researched about this bizarre "syndrome" was true.

When I heard the doctor's voice again, I started coming out of the carnage, which wasn't hard to do because of the bright fluorescent lights above me. I stared at the doctor, thinking how white the lights made his coat. All that stainless steel and rustling white paper pulled across the black vinyl exam table. Now that I was staring at him, I was trying to find some kind of compassion in his face, but he was clinical and to-the-point.

He was a package: neat white coat, well-pressed pants, colour-coordinated tie and shirt, nice leather shoes, and not a strand of hair out of place. I couldn't help think that he was such a young doctor, and yet he didn't seem to have any emotion. I wasn't even sure he was looking at me at all. Maybe someone was controlling him from another office, yet I didn't see any wires. Maybe he was a robot.

I found my notebook and started asking the questions I came prepared with.

He looked surprised. "I see you have been doing a lot of reading."

"Well, there's a big difference from a blood syndrome to cancer, and I didn't get any idea from our first meeting that I was *that* sick."

Dr. Sangfroid went on to explain that he hadn't received all of the pathology reports at our first appointment. Now he could give me the final diagnosis. It was *cancer*.

I could feel myself getting angry, like I had been deceived. Because Bob wasn't hospital savvy and wouldn't know what to ask, my fight-or-flight mode was kicking in full throttle and I started to demand more answers.

"I have this burning and numbness in the ends of my fingers and toes," I continued. "I've looked at all the symptoms for MDS and I don't see anything that would cause this, unless you've had chemo."

"I don't know what would be causing it, but I'll give you a prescription that should help."

"I really don't *want* pills. I'd like to know why I have these symptoms."

He looked up from my chart briefly, shrugged his shoulders and replied, "I don't know."

Dr. Sangfroid was the local hematologist, and I had met him three weeks' previous for the results of my bone marrow biopsy in the outpatient hematology clinic. Bob and I had been sitting in the crowded U-shaped waiting room, laughing and talking about everything except the appointment. I could tell my husband was trying to distract me from the news I was waiting to hear. We talked about his grandson's hockey game and how well his granddaughter was doing in competitive swimming.

That day, when Dr. Sangfroid entered the exam room, he introduced himself and said, "You have myelodysplastic syndrome, which means your bone marrow is older than you are and you'll be transfusion dependent for the rest of your life. Oh, and I've sent your file to oncology. Any questions?"

I wasn't prepared for any of this, and I sat there, stunned. At first I thought he was giving me the

Latin word for the disease. Secondly, I hadn't heard the word *cancer* in anything he said and suddenly he's sending my file to oncology?

My smart mouth, which is a defence mechanism when I'm nervous or scared or don't know what to say, told me to ask: *What the fuck is myelodysplastic syndrome?*

I didn't. Instead, I mumbled meekly, "What's my lifespan expected to be?"

"Well, it could be years, could be decades, have to wait for the rest of the results from your bone marrow test."

Bob could tell I was anticipating the worst, and since the only word we didn't hear was *cancer,* I knew he must have thought everything was fine. Quite frankly, I was hoping the same thing, except the word *oncology* kept bothering me.

"OK, so no other questions?" Dr. Sangfroid asked, breaking the silence. "I'll set you up for a transfusion and a follow-up appointment."

Bob and I walked to the nursing station to book the appointment. To my left were the "lounge chairs" that I'd soon be sitting in to receive my transfusion. Between each seat there were long beige curtains just waiting to be pulled along their tracks to provide much-needed privacy and comfort. Big windows behind each patient let in natural light that would brighten the dullest of days.

"Yes, this is where you will be coming for your transfusion," the nurse booking my next appointment confirmed.

"How long will I be here each time?"

"You can pretty much count on being here for the whole day."

"Will food be provided? What else should I bring?"

"You'll have to bring your own food. Bring electronics, a book, whatever else will keep you occupied for the day."

The next thing I knew we were leaving the hospital and all I could think was, *What the fuck is myelodysplastic syndrome?*

Everyone has heard of some type of cancer: ovarian, breast, prostate, leukemia. I thought I had heard about all of them. But I had never heard of this particular syndrome, and since the word *cancer* was never mentioned, Bob was convinced it wasn't cancer. We didn't even talk about cancer that day. I remember the two of us thinking we had somehow dodged a bullet, that having this blood disease was manageable and didn't sound dire.

I went home that night after my first appointment and called my best friend Sandra in Ottawa. I must have glazed over the details, but she told me later that she'd figured it out right away. Because of either exhaustion or denial, it took four searches on Google before I finally flipped the tablet around for my husband to see.

"What does *this* say?"

"Well, if it was cancer, he would have said it was cancer."

I was not so convinced.

That's why I had suddenly found myself in the cancer clinic for the second appointment. *Duh!* This should have been my first sign that things weren't going to go well, but I was stunned when Dr. Sangfroid told me I had a year to a year and a half to live now that the results of the final tests were in.

So that day when Dr. Sangfroid gave me my new lifespan, my husband and I left the hospital, and I told him I wasn't ready to go home yet. It felt as if I was trying to wake up from a bad dream, and that if we went home right away, it would finalize the diagnosis. One of my dearest friends, Bonnie, is Asian, and she always told me I shouldn't go straight home after a funeral or I would take the souls of the departed with me. Let me tell you, there are a lot of ATMs, gas stations and coffee shops with ghosts hanging around them.

Putting that same theory to use, I told my husband that I wanted to go out for lunch and leave any bad karma from the doctor's office behind. My husband and I went to a restaurant and talked, and I may have even made him laugh. I asked him if he wanted to trade me in now. I still looked pretty good. Wasn't this the reason he was with someone 16 years younger, so I could look after him, not the other way around? Now he was going to have to look after me. I told him now's the time to leave if he wanted to. I was joking, of course. I told him this was the for-better-for-worse part.

This began our healing ritual after every appointment.

CHAPTER 2

Could You Spell
That For Me?

I DID MY DUE DILIGENCE when I returned home after my first appointment in January with Dr. Sangfroid. He had told me he thought my illness was something called myelodysplastic syndrome, or MDS, but he still hadn't explained that it was cancer. I had him spell the syndrome out for me, so I could research it when I got home.

When I started to do my research, I remember thinking that I had been anemic most of my life. I wondered if that was the reason why I had lost my eyelashes.

It was disturbing for me to lose my eyelashes, which happened the fall before I was diagnosed. Not to mention the fact that the hair on my head was starting to grow in like a wire scrub pad. At the time, I attributed it to menopause. I was 52. What did I expect?

Medical professionals believe that MDS starts after a trauma to the body. The patient could have had these mutant cells for years, but it would take a perfect storm for MDS to come to the surface.

That same fall, I had my upper wisdom teeth out and experienced flulike symptoms the next day. By December, I had lost 20 pounds, I was exhausted all the time and I couldn't warm up. I had attributed the exhaustion and coldness to working a lot of overtime at my job as a customs inspector. The weight loss had been gradual, so I didn't notice it until friends pointed it out.

A yearly appointment with a specialist at the end of December and a question regarding how I was feeling in general led me to a routine blood test. Soon after the test, I was called into my GP's office and a bone marrow test was scheduled. All within 10 days.

The way I explain myelodysplastic syndrome to anyone who asks is this: you have kids and you send them off into the world to become productive members of society. Next thing you know they're back at home living in your basement, smoking crack, no job. They don't even help out around the house.

That's the best-case scenario.

Worst-case scenario? They're covered in tattoos, pierced from stem to stern, wearing orange jumpsuits in federal prison. Mine were like that.

That's the way MDS works. Each day our bone marrow produces stem cells. In each stem cell we have what we need to survive: a red blood cell (for oxygen), platelets (for clotting, so we don't bleed to death), and white blood cells (that keep our immune system functioning).

These perfect stem cells are produced every day and if one doesn't mature properly, it is called an "immature cell" or "blast." If the blast count stays low, most likely the prognosis would be favourable and manageable. If the blast count climbs above a certain point, the disease has the potential to have more malignancies and become more aggressive, such as in acute leukemia.

MDS usually attacks one or two out of the three cells in the stem cell, not all three. For me, my red blood cells and white blood cells were compromised. That meant I had no energy and was more likely to catch any cold or disease nearby. I had a high blast

count of seven per cent and was headed for acute my-
elogenous leukemia. The orange-jumpsuit gang had a
hit out on me.

I had my first blood transfusion at the end of
January, and the nurse told me I would be there
all day. So I showed up with a suitcase. The nurses
thought it was hysterical. There had been cutbacks at
the hospital, so I had my own blankets, a change of
clothing and enough food to feed the entire floor.

I arrived at eight in the morning and the nursing
staff was amazing, offering warm blankets and outlets
for my iPad. I thought I was at a spa. I had food for the
day, books to read, my phone, my tablet, and a really
comfy chair. I was pretty much the only person there
for a few hours. A couple of women came in for sim-
pler procedures and left before I finished.

First thing in the morning after I was settled, I
heard the *tap, tap, tap* sound of shoes coming down
the hallway towards me. Who arrives at the nursing
station? Dr. Sangfroid. But not to see me, his only
patient in the transfusion chair. Nope, to talk to the
nurse. He looked my way and gave me a vague smile.
I was the only one there and I'm hooked up intrave-
nously to a bag of blood.

Not even, "Gee, I'm sorry I've forgotten your name, just wanted to check on you. How's your morning going?"

Away he went. Sterile white coat, nice shirt and those pants that are creased so well. This went on all day long, back and forth to the exam room, then to the nurse's station. Not once did he ask how I was doing.

I went through a couple bags of blood and was sent home at the end of the day. I thought I would feel automatically energized, yet I left feeling tired and discouraged. The nurse told me it would take a few days to a week before I would start seeing any changes.

CHAPTER 3

Bedazzled

IT'S OFFICIAL. I'M A PATIENT at the cancer clinic.

My nurse, Nurse Merry, had just called to give me the results of the blood work I had to have done weekly, and then said she wanted to talk to me about "Vidaza."

"What's that?" I asked.

"Oh, it's a low-dose chemo drug given by injections. You wouldn't have to stay in the chemo suite. You'd just come in and get the injection and leave. You get so many doses, and then there's a break, and then you start up again. It's very low risk."

Merry had a way of talking that always made me want to scream. Every time she called, it was like nails on a chalkboard. It was partly her voice, but also her demeanour. You can be pleasant and professional, but this woman was *way too happy* to be making phone calls from the cancer clinic. She'd call to talk to me about chemo and I felt like she was trying to talk me into purchasing a magazine subscription.

Stunned is probably a good way to describe how I was feeling. Dr. Sangfroid didn't say anything about chemo at our last appointment.

Nurse Merry continued: "It will probably be at least a week before we start."

She gave me the correct spelling of the drug, so I could look it up and find out exactly what it would do to me, and what side effects I might experience while taking it.

The Internet is a great tool, but you also have to know when to get off the highway of information. I looked up the chemotherapy drug azacitidine, or Vidaza, as it's more commonly known, and Nurse Merry had been accurate. The side effects were low, but what I didn't understand was the expected outcome of this type of chemo.

You see, by this time my red blood cells (the ones that give you oxygen and energy) were already in the crapper. My white blood cells and neutrophils (both keep your immune system up and running) were also almost nonexistent.

I didn't understand what Dr. Sangfroid expected this chemo drug to do. Explaining didn't seem to be his strong suit. All of a sudden I have a year to live, and then without any explanation I'm getting a mild form of chemo. Details to follow?

I knew there wasn't a chemotherapy drug that could go in and only eradicate cancer cells. There was going to be collateral damage. Because I was so weak by this point, I was concerned I wouldn't be able to handle a procedure that would drain any more of my energy.

Afterwards, I met with my mom for lunch and explained that the doctor told me I had a blood disorder requiring transfusions for the rest of my life. I had been anemic on and off since I was a child, so she didn't push any further.

I decided not to mention the chemo. Not then. But the fact that this was becoming a reality might become a problem because of our small community. To add to the situation, Sault Ste. Marie is a border crossing where I worked as a customs officer, and my mom and I would often go to the U.S. for lunch. What if one of my former coworkers saw me and asked if I had started my treatment yet?

That wasn't the way I wanted her to find out.

We went out for lunch again and I slowly explained a few more pieces of the puzzle. I still *never* told her the doctor had given me a certain life expectancy or such a short amount of time to live.

She started to tear up. My mother is a strong woman with a great sense of humour, and I could tell that this had taken some light out of her eyes. She dropped me off at home and I promised I would be fine.

That same week I had an appointment with my family doctor, Dr. Kevin. Every time I saw him it felt like I was showing up at a dorm room at Harvard. He always wore preppy clothing—plaid shirts, khaki pants—like he just graduated from university.

Dr. Kevin took my illness seriously from the beginning. He was the one who booked my bone marrow biopsy test after my first set of blood work.

When I questioned why he was getting his shorts in a knot about the results of my blood work, he said, "I think it's some type of blood cancer."

"Get the fuck out of here."

Dr. Kevin had always been forthright about what he thought was going on. I had already mentioned the numbness and the burning I was experiencing in my feet and hands, and he was genuinely concerned.

Now I had come to see him regarding an eye problem: I couldn't see out of my left eye. It was completely blurry. I had noticed it the night before while I was trying to bake. I had the iPad set up in the kitchen and felt like there was something in my right eye. When I closed it, I couldn't read a thing with my left. Are you fucking kidding me?

Dr. Kevin had me read the eye chart in his office, but because he didn't think it was a comprehensive enough test, referred me to my regular optometrist, who told me it was a cataract, but to be sure sent me to the ophthalmologist, who then told me I had road rash. How the hell did I get road rash in my eye?

Getting ready to leave, I told him that Dr. Sangfroid wanted to start me on chemo.

"You can ask for a second opinion, you know," Dr. Kevin stated matter-of-factly.

"Really?" I asked.

Up until this point, I didn't realize I had any choice with my treatments. I always believed that the doctor knew best. Now I felt like I was learning how to fight for myself and for my health.

The next morning I called Nurse Merry and told her they could start chemo, but I wanted a second opinion.

"Oh," she stammered. "Just a minute."

She put me on hold for a couple of minutes and then said that Dr. Sangfroid wanted to see me.

When I got off the phone, I started thinking that he must want to talk to me about the side effects of the chemo and tell me that it wouldn't cause much damage, *yadi yadi yada*. I was surprised at how fast I was able to get in to see him, so I prepared my questions for the appointment.

Back on the highway of information, I tried to find the best resources to make sure I didn't feel insecure or unprepared when I headed into my next appointment. There were so many websites and so much help out there, but my go-to place was the Mayo Clinic website. Their information is accurate and professional, with a section that helps you prepare questions for your appointment.

In I went to see Dr. Sangfroid, and the first thing out of his mouth was, "We aren't going to give you *Vi-DAY-za*."

My mouth dropped open. "You aren't going to give me *Vi-DAZZ-za*? I have three pages of questions for you."

"It's *Vi-DAY-za!*"

"Oh, that's too bad, I thought it was *Vi-DAZZ-za*, which sounded like *bedazzled*, and I thought I was going to be all bedazzled when I was done, you know?"

Nothing, just a blank look on his face.

Now I started talking even faster, which happens a lot when people don't answer me.

"Like all blingy, you know? Didn't you ever hear about them when you were young? Not that you would have used one, but you know, you put crystal studs in a gun and you can put them on anything, a jacket, a belt, makes you all sparkly. That's what I thought this chemo would do. I'd be all blingy and sparkly!"

He looked at me and he looked at Bob and said, "I got nothing."

Really? Not even a smile. Nothing?

Dr. Sangfroid continued: "I brought you in here today because we aren't going to be giving you chemo anymore. We are going to put you on the list for a stem cell transplant because it will be a *cure*."

Cure. *Ding, ding, ding.* We have a winner here. Did he just say *cure*? How the hell is that possible?

He continued to tell us that he discussed it with the stem cell transplant unit at the hospital in Ottawa, and because my myelodysplastic syndrome was so far advanced, and yet I was still in fairly good health and a good age, the bone marrow transplant team felt it was a better course of action.

Because it would probably be at least six to eight weeks to find a donor, I would still be monitored in Sault Ste. Marie while waiting for the transplant to take place in Ottawa.

Wait a minute. So I ask for a second opinion and now you're going to cure me? Two weeks ago you were going to give me chemo. Are you kidding me?

All the time he was talking, my thoughts were wandering back to the fact that if I hadn't asked for a second opinion, I would be receiving chemo right now. Five bucks says not looking very blingy either.

So that's how it works. From that point on, I had every *medical professional* explain what was going on, the reasons why I needed what they were trying to give me, and why they were doing what they were doing.

I felt like I was still climbing out of more wreckage. *I am not this stupid*, I kept saying to myself. Yet I kept getting blindsided. Well, it was going to stop. I don't know how people do it, especially those who are sicker or don't have advocates to help them out. Some of them probably die. That fact scared me, and so from that point on, I paid attention to every little detail.

I found it was important to keep notes of every appointment, and to get copies of every file and form. I wanted to understand and research everything that was going on with me. As often as I could, I had someone come with me to every appointment to make sure I didn't miss anything, and to reassure me that I wasn't losing my mind. You can be sure there were days when I felt like I *had* lost it.

That day was the start of a whole new adventure for me.

CHAPTER 4

If It's Cracked, Maybe We Should Fix It

ONCE I RECEIVED THE NEWS about the stem cell transplant, it felt like an enormous amount of pressure was building up around me, and it was going to hit like a tsunami. There were so many things to do to get ready. I had to pack, fill out paperwork, make reservations, and see people before I left.

While it was difficult to read my family, my friends Sandra and Bonnie were excited that there was a cure, and they couldn't wait for me to get to Ottawa, where they both live. I knew Sandra could keep me calm, and I knew if I didn't have any energy left, Bonnie would be stacking bodies like cordwood if I didn't get the proper treatment.

I was starting to notice that my immediate family was having a hard time with the fact that I was sick. Reflecting back on it now—after months of counselling—I was angry, but I wasn't letting anyone know how to help me.

I would have the stem cell transplant done at the Bone Marrow Transplant unit, or BMT for short, at the Ottawa Hospital. They had just called to schedule the pre-transplant testing at my local hospital for the following week.

That was the first weekend of March and it was March Break. You could almost feel the pressure in the air building up when my husband got out of bed that Saturday morning.

I could hear sniffing and coughing sounds in the bathroom, like his nose was running, and I thought to myself, *Oh please, not again, not now. I don't have the strength to deal with this too.*

About 18 months before, Bob had had a huge nose-bleed called a posterior nosebleed, which bleeds from the back of the throat. It was so bad that by the time I entered the bathroom, he looked like there had been a hit ordered by the Mafia in our mostly white bathroom. I finally made him hang his head over the tub. I wouldn't even let my mother go in when she came to let our dogs out that day.

On this particular morning, he finally came back to bed.

Are you alright?" I asked, hoping everything was fine.

"Yeah, I think so."

He barely got back into bed when he started bleeding again. He made a beeline for the washroom and I stumbled out of bed on his tail. When I got there, blood was gushing into the sink.

I looked at him and asked, "Ambulance again?"

"Yep."

The ambulance came to get him, and at the hospital a nice young female doctor wanted to try and pack his nose, and to try this and that.

I went and got a tea, and when I came back I offered a suggestion: "You have to put a balloon in. It's the only thing that works with him."

She took out two packages to show me: "Which one?"

"The one that looks like a baby penis."

"Are you a paediatric nurse?"

"No, just been here lots of times and bought several T-shirts."

She kind of chuckled.

I settled Bob in a room and started my daily treks back and forth to the hospital the next day.

While waiting for the transplant, the BMT also had me booked for chemo teaching, CAT scan, pulmonary function test and an ECG, plus extra blood work.

Because I wasn't supposed to have any chemo before the transplant, the cancer unit tried to cancel my chemo teaching class, but I asked if I could still attend because I would ultimately get chemo right before the stem cell transplant.

This session was a great source of information for me. The hospital had a detailed binder specifically for each one of us, depending on what type of cancer and treatment we would receive. There is no such thing as too much information.

This class gave me many resources to deal with other issues that were going on at the time. Because I was already immune-supressed, they taught us ways to stay healthy during and after our chemo treatments. They provided a recipe for a throat rinse I still use to this day, as well as suggested foods to help control the nausea. It was the most comprehensive information I had been given so far.

I completed all of the testing and the class while visiting my husband in the hospital. My hemoglobin was extremely low, and at the end of each day I was done like dinner.

Bob spent a week in the hospital, and a procedure that should have taken 20 minutes turned into an hour and a half. We ended up looking like a scene from *Weekend at Bernie's* because I had to drag him stoned on morphine from one facility to another to get the procedure done, and I was so weak I could barely get him up the wheelchair ramp.

When he was ready to go home, a sweet young nurse said to him,"You should go home and have a nice steak with all the blood you've lost."

Yeah, that's what I'm thinking. I'll make a fucking pot roast and potatoes.

We no sooner get home and I'm going out to get his prescription filled when he said to me, "Maybe it would be nice to have a steak."

"You're fucking kidding me right now, aren't you?"

"But I'm so weak."

"Welcome to my world for the last few months."

At the pharmacy the pharmacist said," Oh, no, is Bob sick too?"

"Yes, he had one of those awful nosebleeds, so I'm going to make him steak and arsenic for supper!"

The pharmacist turned red and didn't know what to say.

"Just joking. I don't actually have arsenic."

She reached for the little white bag of pills quickly. "Ah, here's Bob's prescription."

Great, now I look like a psychopath, and a very pale psychopath at that.

My sick leave from customs ended the third week of March and the disability documents started to fly. I'm the one who fills in everything for the two of us. Bob had no idea how to help me, and the two friends I would have trusted to complete these details, Bonnie and Sandra, were in Ottawa.

I felt a hairline crack forming. I kept thinking, *Who applies for disability just for fun?* I was overwrought with paperwork. On top of that, the numbness and burning in the ends of my fingers made it excruciatingly difficult to write or type anything.

There were mountains of forms to fill out and a strange feeling in the air. One night I went down to our garage, which is attached to our house under our living room, and I could see a huge gaping crack on the far wall staring back at me.

I called Bob down: "Look!"

"What do you think is going to happen?" he asked nonchalantly.

I stared at him incredulously and said, "I think we're going to be like that poor family just outside of Montreal. They were watching an NHL game and their house collapsed into a sinkhole. The only one that survived was the golden retriever because he was tied up outside."

I could feel my voice rising. "The one wall is raised away from the other one, Bob. Maybe we should fix it?"

"OK, I'll get a waterproofing guy in."

A few days later, the waterproofing guy comes and says, "Whoa, buddy, I can't fix that. You need an engineer."

That was the start of the collapse. And not just the house.

By *collapse,* I mean that it was very difficult for my husband to try and figure out how to deal with our major structural issue and my major health crisis.

Now that we've dealt with these issues, Bob and I have talked about the fact that counselling was never offered to either one of us. Counselling is vital. I filled out the request in a hospital form, but I didn't hear back from anyone.

It's hard enough being the patient, but caregivers aren't given enough support or guidance. Especially when the roles are reversed. I have always been healthy and now Bob had to look after me. To make matters worse, I didn't know how to ask for help.

Healthcare should be all-encompassing to get us through these difficult times. Communication is key. This is not the time to shut down. There has to be a dialogue at all times, if not with our spouses, then with friends and family. Better yet, speak with a counsellor. If you can manage it, try and find some humour in your situation. Believe it or not, you can always find something that will make you laugh.

CHAPTER 5

Should You Be Drinking?

AT THIS POINT, RINGLING BROS. could have hired me to be one of their jugglers.

There was a structural crack in the house, with its own host of characters—engineers, city officials and insurance people. Then there were the numerous tests I had to get done. Not to mention paperwork up the wazoo.

Finally, the first week of April I had a video conference at our local hospital with the oncologist from the Bone Marrow Transplant unit in Ottawa.

I decided to bring both my husband and my mother to the video conference with me because they needed to understand what a stem cell transplant was and what I would be dealing with. Despite several books I had brought home from my class, I felt they both thought the transplant was going to be something like a vaccine. I believed that neither of them really heard any of the other details after the word *cure*.

We headed to the hospital and into the room where the conference was being held. It was like I was back in high school. The door reminded me of one of my English classes, and we actually sat at desks set up for us. Oh my God, I was 16 again, and I automatically wanted to chew gum and stick it underneath the desk before I left. I had my mom on one side of me, my husband on the other.

When the video conference finally started, the doctor bustled onto the screen and appeared to be more concerned with the fact that he hadn't had his hair cut before our appointment. He repeatedly apologized while trying to straighten his outdated '80s hairstyle. After running his hands through his hair for several minutes and making it look like he had just arrived by helicopter, Dr. DeVain launched into a diatribe about what was going to be my reality in a few weeks.

I kept interrupting to ask questions because I knew I'd forget them, and he became flustered, like I'd interrupted his oral presentation. Which was when he asked me if I could wait until he was finished his speil. Well, he didn't say *speil*. I said that. He actually said that he had a certain way of describing the transplant and he would like to say it and then I could ask my questions.

Finally, he was finished and I started with my questions again.

"Will I lose my hair?"

"Not right away, but when you have the transplant you will because of the level of chemo."

"Perfect. I already have a haircut picked out!"

He laughed.

"Do you know anything about this numbness I have in my fingers, which has now spread to my calves? Dr. Sangfroid doesn't seem to know what it is."

"No," Dr. DeVain replied.

I was trying to keep the questions to a minimum because, out of my peripheral vision, I could tell that Bob and my mother looked like they'd been hit by a semi-truck. I knew they had both been shocked by the 40 per cent survival rate. I had already learned about this from my chemo class and had time to absorb the dire statistic. Don't ask me why, but it didn't concern me. I just knew I would be alright.

I had not been surprised by a thing the doctor had told me, aside from the fact that I would have to stay in Ottawa for at least a couple of months after the transplant to make sure that my body wouldn't reject the donor cells.

My mother became more involved when we were asked about siblings.

"Yes, she has a brother," my mother said proudly. Like she was announcing there was a superhero in the family.

She had a puzzled look on her face when Dr. DeVain went on to tell her they would test my brother to see if he was a match, but the odds of a stranger being a match were much greater. My mother could not comprehend this, even though I had tried to get her to read the transplant books I had brought home. In them, they explained if you had only one sibling, it was a one-in-four chance he or she would be a donor match. The Bone Marrow Donor Registry would likely be more helpful because there are currently millions of registrants to draw from.

We left the hospital, and Bob and I took my mother back to her apartment. She had been quiet during the drive, but finally spoke when she was getting out of the car.

"Gee, that was a lot to take in. I'm taking a pot of stew out to your brother's and I'll call you later."

"Yes, it was a lot of information," I replied.

That was when one of my anger bubbles surfaced during my illness. It took me a long time to comprehend why my family couldn't look after me.

I remember saying to my husband that day: "She's taking stew to my brother? They told me I have a 40 per cent survival rate and she's taking *him* stew? Are you fucking kidding me?"

I knew my brother had his own problems going on and my mom felt like she could help him, whereas she didn't know what to do for me. He was going through a nasty breakup, and the grandson she adored and babysat almost daily she now hadn't seen in weeks.

I also knew that taking both my husband and my mother to the video conference was going to be difficult. I had read everything I could get my hands on because I wanted to know what I was up against. Now I felt I had given everyone a false sense of hope.

I saw a change in both my husband and my mother that day. After dropping off my mother, I thought to myself, *I'm not going straight home after hearing all that crap.*

"I want to go out for supper," I said, looking at Bob. "Besides, we have to discuss wig options."

I had always told my husband that if I lost my hair, he would never know which woman he was coming home to on a daily basis. It was bad enough over the years when I used to change my hairstyle quarterly, now he could sleep with a new woman *every* night. I think by then he thought I had lost my mind, and he rolled his eyes, which is what he does when I say outrageous things and he doesn't know whether to take me seriously or not.

We went to this great little Italian restaurant because I wanted ricotta gnocchi and they have the best. When we arrived, the owner came over to talk to us for a while, sent us a complementary appetizer, and we settled in with drinks.

"Well, were you surprised by anything today?" I asked.

"Yes, how long you had to be in isolation and how long you had to stay in Ottawa."

"Why didn't you read any of the material I brought home?"

"I don't know," he replied.

Sadly, I think he thought that if he just waited a little longer, maybe none of this would be true. I told him I would be fine. I was just going to go and get it done and be back home.

It was just what we both needed that night. Delicious Italian food and a table close to the fireplace, which filled the room with a warm glow. When we went back home, we felt calmer and laughed that we had left not only the dirty dishes behind, but all the negative energy as well.

Even though some of the information I received at the video conference surprised me—that I was going to have to be in isolation longer than I thought, and that I was going to have to stay in Ottawa longer than I thought—some of the information I was prepared for.

I knew I was going to have a Port-A-Cath inserted in my upper chest, which is a better choice for patients who require frequent chemotherapy, blood transfusions, antibiotics, intravenous feeding or blood withdrawals. This was one of the things I was going to insist upon. I didn't want a catheter in my arm because it is much more difficult to get your clothing on and off, and to bathe.

So what do you do with that information? You go online shopping, of course. I started ordering dresses accessible for the catheter, and because one of my symptoms was that my balance was off, flat, comfortable shoes so I could stay upright. I shopped like I was going to a resort. Fuck it. I figured if I had to stay anywhere for that length of time, I was going to look good. I was going to rock that isolation unit. Look good, heal faster, right?

I called my hairdresser and made an appointment to have my shoulder-length hair cut short. I had already started looking at wigs and was in the process of figuring out what style I was going to go with and how many I wanted. I had all kinds of new identities picked out: a long blonde wig I would call Grace, a fun red bob called Natasha, and finally, Lana, a shoulder-length number with lots of curls. (I probably watched too many old movies with my grandmother when I was a little girl.)

Those were only the first few wigs I had picked out. I couldn't believe how many there were, and just like shoes, I could have the same style in every colour. The Internet becomes dangerous when your energy is low and you aren't able to get out of the house. Bob's granddaughter Halle was over one evening and she helped me pick out some items. I think she may have restrained me a little.

Next step, a haircutting party! Bob's daughter-in-law arranged a lunch with some of my coworkers, friends and relatives to meet after my hair appointment.

That morning, after I had arrived at the salon, my two friends and coworkers, Caroline and Tina, came to hold my hand as the hairdresser "did the dirty deed."

My neighbour down the street, who went through chemo himself, advised against cutting my hair too short because it would be itchy. Never thought about that.

It was a good point, but I knew it would be easier emotionally if I cut my hair now rather than wait until the chemo kicked in, when my beautiful auburn hair would start to fall out like needles on an old Christmas tree. I had already decided on a short '70s style and made the appointment.

Tasha, my hairdresser, who is blond and beautiful and like a daughter to me, later told me that cutting my hair might have been harder on her than it was on me.

That was probably true. I tried to see every step of this as an adventure. Caroline, who is my dear friend, can recite movie clips or remember funny things that happened at work, and she kept us in stitches through the whole appointment. It was exactly what I needed. I might have even peed my pants from laughing so hard, but with the numbness, I couldn't tell.

Later, we went for lunch at a local restaurant. Some of my friends met us there. Maria, whom I ride motorcycles with, and my cousin Patti, who is an organ transplant recipient and a godsend to me because of what she has gone through both emotionally and physically.

We laughed hysterically about arguing with Siri when trying to call a friend or a business. The voice is so polite, and then you feel road rage because you've asked for an address and Siri says it isn't in your contacts when you know damn well it's there. Then she pronounces it with an accent that sounds like it's between two languages and you end up cursing at her.

The three of us who had worked at customs together were talking about wild things that had happened to us over the years—you can't imagine what people will try to smuggle over the border—and of course we all talked about our kids and the things they had done to make us laugh. All while enjoying a copious amount of food. It made the day complete.

Two weeks later, I scheduled an appointment for a wig fitting. I looked at it as another adventure. I took my mom and her friend Alyce, and Bob's granddaughter Halle. I figured it wouldn't hurt to have some objective opinions since I was liable to come home with hooker hairpieces.

When we arrived at the salon, my mother looked like she would rather be anywhere else. I know now, after counselling, how difficult that afternoon was for her. I was trying to make light of the fact that I needed a wig, but I could tell by the look in her eyes that this had made the diagnosis a reality. At the time, I felt angry and hurt that she wasn't able to help, while Alyce and Halle were giving me more valuable advice.

In the end, I chose a very different wig than what I went in for. My colouring had changed because my hemoglobin was so low, so I couldn't get the wig I thought I wanted.

That afternoon, I brought Danielle home in a box. Up until this point, I had been a redhead. Danielle had rich chocolate shoulder-length hair with caramel highlights. She was my first alter ego.

You have to have a bit of imagination and fun when you're going through something like this. I had lost 25 per cent of my hearing because of the sounds of the airbrakes resonating in the booth while I was stationed as a customs officer and now wore two hearing aids. Then I'm told I'm dying.

Seriously, some patent-leather thigh-high hooker boots were looking good. That's probably why some of my next purchases were a couple of Wonder Woman and YOLO (You Only Live Once) T-shirts.

Most days, my energy was terrible, but I felt I needed to keep pushing myself in order to believe everything was going to be fine. It made me think if I put on a good show, I could make everyone around me believe it too. If I didn't manage to get out, I would plan to have lunch or have someone come and get me, so I had something to look forward to.

Then, one day I went out in the early afternoon to do some paperwork, and I hadn't been gone long because I remember taking my two dogs, Molly and Theo, with me in the car. Molly is a golden retriever and Theo is a Bernedoodle. Theo is my little—actually really huge—boy, and since I had become sick and been at home more, he was especially attached to me. He loves getting out of the house and I felt bad that I couldn't always get him out to throw a ball or take him for a walk. Molly was in her "golden" years and really could care less for outdoor activities, but she was always up for a car ride.

By the time I got back I was exhausted. I remember thinking I probably shouldn't be driving because I was so tired. I couldn't believe how much a short car ride could take such a physical and emotional toll on me.

I loved driving, I had been a driving instructor for years, and all I could think about on the way home was, *Is there a light at this corner? Is there a stop sign? Holy shit, I have to think about this.*

That was a wakeup call for me. After that, I didn't drive if I was tired or stressed out.

When I got home, all I wanted to do was relax, maybe make a drink and a snack. I don't normally drink alcohol in the afternoon, but I was so rattled when I returned home, I thought it couldn't make things any worse. So I mixed a drink, made a nice little plate with tomatoes and cheese and crackers, sat on the couch, and enjoyed the beautiful view. Our house is set into the side of a hill, and we overlook the entire city: the arches of the International Bridge, the river.

The phone rang. It was my mom.

"How are you feeling?" she asked.

"I'm really tired."

"What are you doing?"

"I'm having a drink and a snack."

Silence. Dead air.

"Mom, you still there?"

"Should you be drinking?"

I started to laugh hysterically. "You're fucking kidding me, right? You're lucky I don't have a meth lab in the garage or a grow-op in the laundry room. I'm just having a drink."

I was also thinking, *Or doing acid or a line of coke. Or some of the really risky behaviours I had heard about growing up but didn't do.* Not that I think I missed anything.

"Well, what did the doctor say about drinking?"

"I'm not asking the doctor about drinking. Are you kidding me? I have cancer. How much worse could a drink make it?"

CHAPTER 6

You Gotta Have Friends

MY FRIENDS BASICALLY HELPED ME through my illness.

"But you chose them," my husband said.

"Yes, I did, because I needed to know I had people who were going to get me through this. At the time, you were dealing with the garage, my mom was dealing with my brother, and my brother was dealing with his own problems. Nobody was capable of dealing with the reality that I might die."

I realize now that if I'd had counselling from the beginning, I could've explained my needs to my family, but I didn't know how to do that at the time.

I found that when I was dealing with MDS, I needed lots of friends and my extended family. My immediate family wanted to keep me safe and at home, which made me feel smothered. Not to mention insane.

So I called Sandra and Bonnie in Ottawa, who were going to look after me when I had the transplant done.

Kellie, who lives in Colorado, let me be myself. An accomplished pilot, she would always let me tag along with her when she went flying. To this day, my favourite trip is the one she and I took in a World War II military trainer known as a Harvard.

We are psychically connected and seem to know when one or the other is feeling off. If I wanted to talk about being sick, she was OK with that. If I didn't, she was fine with that too. That was important to me. Having friends like that allowed me to get out of bed and move forward each day.

I also had to have a game plan or something to do each day. Caroline and Tina took me for lunch, to the movies, or to their house for tea so I wouldn't have a bad day.

Then there were my motorcycle girlfriends, Maria and Deb. If I didn't hear from Deb one day, I'd hear from Maria, and vice versa.

I had a posse of women from U.S. customs who would meet me for supper at least once a month, and they still keep in touch. They filled me in on what was going on at work, and made me feel like I hadn't stopped working with them.

Most of my friends helped in so many ways: phone calls, cards, flowers. The support kept coming and I was grateful.

It felt like I never stopped, but when I think about it, I usually went out once a day and that was enough. I had to keep going mentally. The next day I usually slept the whole day away. I think it made my husband crazy. When I wasn't sleeping, I had plans to do something. Not that I always followed through with them; it just made me feel alive.

My friend Shirin called one day from her beautiful inn on Manitoulin Island and asked if I would like to come for a visit. I wasn't having a particularly good week and asked if she would call back another time.

"Absolutely, baby."

When I told Bob that she had called, he said, "You're not going there, you're too tired, *yadi yadi yada*…."

I just glared at him. "I will go where I want and when. Besides, you didn't even ask me what I said to her."

"Well, what did you say?"

"I told her not right now, maybe in a couple of weeks."

Sure enough, a couple of weeks later she drove over five hours to bring me back to Meldrum Bay on Manitoulin Island, which is heaven on Earth for me. She and her husband Bob own the Meldrum Bay Inn and it is such a tranquil place. The island can only be accessed by ferry or rail bridge, and once you're on the island, Meldrum is at the end of the highway. If you're lucky, you can get cell service.

People come this way either because they're lost or they're looking for the end of the rainbow. There is water all around and the hummingbirds never stop. The inn's veranda was there long before the roads were built, and you can sit on the porch with a cup of coffee, a good meal or a drink, and enjoy the scenery, which is both relaxing and cathartic.

Being on Meldrum was just what I needed at the time, and Shirin treated me like royalty while I was there. Every day she had breakfast ready. She also made me lamb marrow cooked in a pressure cooker, which she said would heal my own marrow. We had to negotiate on the prunes in a glass mug, however. They looked like dried-up sheep's testicles, and we had to put lots of hot water in that mug before I would touch them.

Shirin is a wise woman, and she knew I needed to get away from all the phone calls and questions. When I returned, I felt renewed, and it gave me enough strength to keep moving forward.

I did the same thing about a month and a half later with my friend Michele. It was probably the last trip I drove anywhere on my own. Michele, who shares my passion for motorcycles, lives in Boyne, Michigan. We met at Lady Biker Day six years ago, and we became fast friends, travelling together to the Harley-Davidson Factory in Milwaukee, Wisconsin, where we took a basic motorcycle mechanics course.

She was another friend I hadn't seen in a while and she had called with an open-ended invitation. When you are given a timeline and there are friends out of town whom you think you might not see again, I had to pack my bag and go.

I should be grateful I didn't give my husband a stroke. I remember getting up that morning and checking my blood pressure because I was so tired, and the machine wouldn't register anything. Checked it again and it was 85 over 57. I didn't tell Bob. I just went back to bed for a couple of hours and then got on the road.

Instead of taking the Interstate, I took the back roads, thinking that at least I could go at a slower pace, and get off and take a nap if I needed to. I could tell when I got there that Michele was both shocked and happy to see me. I kept forgetting how bad I looked. I knew I was pale and down 20 pounds, but when she opened the door, the look on her face. Well, let's just say it's a good thing I didn't say, "Boo."

I feel like I'm her sister when I go to visit. We like to sit around and have a drink and chat about our family and friends, where we would like to travel, and of course, our motorcycles. It's like we've known each other forever.

Her husband, Tom, and her dog, Lucky, also make me feel especially welcome, except that Lucky's idea of making me feel at home is going for a swim in the lake and then lying down on the guest pillow until he dries. He's hilarious, giving me the old stink eye, as if he were about to say to me: "Sick or not, you're interrupting one-on-one time with *my* parents."

I stayed four days and sat in the sun, listened to the water lap against the shore, and watched the sun set.

These trips gave me the strength to realize what I knew all along. You gotta have friends, and I'd be around to see them for a long time to come.

CHAPTER 7

Put Your Own Oxygen Mask On First

I HAD BEEN STOIC WITH everyone and hadn't cried when the doctor told me I was going to die. My one weak spot—and I don't mean that ironically—was the fact that I couldn't get back on my motorcycle. Our garage is attached to the house, so I had to pass it every time I went out. Now that the garage needed to be fixed, the bike had to be moved, so it was going to my good friend and co-worker Don's house, and he would take it for a spin once in a while over the summer.

Slowly my independence was slipping away. I let people pick me up from lunch more often, let my husband do more of the driving. Now the bike wasn't even going to be there so I could at least convince myself I would ride again.

The night before Donnie was to come and get the bike, I went down to the garage to take the day bag off and some things out of the saddlebags. When I came back up, it was clear that I had been crying.

"What's the matter with you?" Bob asked.

"Donnie's coming to get the bike tomorrow."

"So? It's just temporary."

I knew he didn't understand how I felt. Not being able to ride my motorcycle that summer was worse than dying for me. Knowing I wouldn't see my bike every day left me feeling empty.

I went into survival mode. Time to put my own oxygen mask on first. I called friends and a couple of cousins I knew I could talk to.

For anyone going through any type of illness, it has taken me a year to get over my anger. If your immediate family or good friends don't step up to the plate, sometimes it's because they aren't physically or emotionally capable of dealing with the situation. Their dinner plates might be too full, or you haven't asked for help. I have also realized that sometimes friends and relatives once removed have an easier time dealing with situations like this. They have more clarity and a little distance from the emotional side of things.

So when it came time to get testing done to see if my brother and I were a match for the bone marrow, the BMT unit had to send a kit to him. Two weeks later I called my brother about it.

"Did you hear anything? Did you get the kit?"

"No," he snapped at me.

"Well, it's been a couple of weeks."

"I haven't seen it, Karen. It must have gotten lost."

Now, you have to understand, the bone marrow unit would not go to the universal list of donors until my brother had been ruled out. So I called Katie, the co-ordinator of the BMT unit in Ottawa, who said, "Well, I don't know where it is."

All I heard in my head was *tick tock, tick tock*. Patience is definitely not my strong suit.

"Well, can't we just have a blood test done at the local hospital?" I asked.

"Sure," she said. "I can't see any reason why not."

Well, you think I was trying to get blood from the Holy Father himself. Nobody had a clue how to do this at our local hospital. Just one more thing that was frustrating and demoralizing.

When people don't have the strength or the energy to deal with their own health crises, there needs to be a patient advocacy system set up to guide them through each procedure and test so patients feel well-informed about their treatment options.

But I'm digressing. So I called someone I knew at the hospital.

"What the fuck is going on that I can't get a blood test set up for my brother? This isn't a regular blood test; this is to see if he is going to be a match for my stem cell. I'll tell you what's going to happen. First thing in the morning we're going to be at the lab and someone is going to take his blood!"

"Don't go all code white on us," she laughed.

"What's that?"

"That's when security has to come and have you physically removed."

That's when I called my brother on my Bluetooth to see which day he could go to the hospital.

This is what he said to me: "Today I have my lawyer's appointment. Tomorrow I have my son."

"What about Monday?"

Wait for it....

"Monday. Oh, I have to take the dog to the vet."

I was quiet for a few seconds. "You do understand that this is a matter of life and death, eh?"

Then he started to get angry at *me*, so I hung up. I phoned my son and started to cry. I knew I couldn't call my mother because she would be caught in the middle. I couldn't go home and tell my husband. If I did, I was pretty sure we'd have the blood sample that afternoon.

CHAPTER 8

Number Than a Stump!

ON THE UPSIDE, NO BRAIN tumour. My GP, Dr. Kevin, was beside himself because the numbness that had started in my hands and feet was now up to my waist. He'd had me sent for an MRI. He also called and begged, pleaded and cajoled, and managed to get me into our new neurologist, Dr. Gentil.

Bob went with me to the appointment and a young Norwegian god walked in. All I could think of was, *Holy shit, he's so good-looking. Blond wavy hair I would love to run my hands through, high chiselled cheekbones you could cut your hands on, and gorgeous blue eyes you could drown in.*

Wait, this can't be the doctor. Sure as shit, he put his hand out to shake mine and all I could think was,

Maybe I could execute an arm-bar takedown right now and put him on the floor.... Oh, nice thought, but don't think you could wrestle your way out of a wet paper bag, girl.

"Mrs. Zachary? I'm Dr. Gentil. I'm just going to get you to change into an exam gown and I'll be right back."

I'll just take everything off right here right now. I don't need an exam gown.

Oh, wait, my husband's here.

As soon as the doctor left the examination room, I turned to my husband and said, "Sorry, honey. He's gorgeous."

"I just want his hair," replied Bob, who has been follicly challenged for most of his later years.

"Your doctor must think there is something really wrong with you," Dr. Gentil said when he came back in. "There's a three-month waiting period to get in to see me."

"He does, so do I."

He started talking to me again and the entire time I'm thinking, *He's the whole package. He's nice, kind, sweet, takes his time. He's thorough, doesn't make me feel like I'm taking up his time. Looks me in the eyes.*

He put me through some tests and agreed with me, that there wasn't any way I could have two issues going on at the same time, especially since I never had chemo. He filled in a lab request for blood work and added test names at the bottom—copper, zinc, B6, B12, and a few others. In all, there were 15 blood tests. I went right that afternoon to have the tests done, although some of the tests had to be sent away. I took photocopies of everything.

The last week of June we headed to Ottawa for my pre-transplant clinic. Bob and I were staying with Sandra and her husband, Dave. My other good friend Bonnie, the one who was to be "my person" at the hospital, was coming to meet us at the house.

It was funny when I told Sandra I had chosen Bonnie to be "my person" and that I was also staying with her after the isolation.

"Why can't *I* be your person?" Sandra asked.

"OK, you can be my other person."

So the next day I called her at work. Voicemail. I called her later on. Voicemail. The next day, same thing.

When I finally got a hold of her, I said, "That's why you can't be my person. I keep getting your voicemail. I get Bonnie on the first ring. When I need you, I need you."

We laughed. Sandra is my gentle, send-me-a-Gund-teddy-bear, even-tempered friend. Her voice is always the same whether I call her at one o'clock in the afternoon or one in the morning. I can call in an absolute rage or feel like I am on the precipice of doing something not particularly helpful to myself and she will help me to see it isn't wise. This is probably why she's such a good boss.

Dave was the chef and the chauffeur, but when it comes to driving, he's hell on wheels. On a positive note, it was the one thing that reminded me I was alive each and every time he drove me to an appointment.

Bonnie, on the other hand, is very organized and well-acquainted with the hospital environment, since within the previous nine months she had lost three close family members, including her husband, who not only had been a friend of ours, but also one of our coworkers at customs in the Sault.

She was very protective of me. I knew she would ask the same questions I would ask and demand the answers, or else.

I should explain that Bob, Sandra, Dave, Bonnie and I have all known each other for almost 30 years. We worked as customs officers together, and now they were coming with me to the hospital to be my first-class interrogation team.

Sandra and Dave, along with my husband and I, have done quite a bit of travelling together since they moved to Ottawa. Bonnie and I kind of lost touch but reconnected in 2013 when I knew she was experiencing loss of her own. By the time I arrived in Ottawa that June, she had gone through a lot of grieving, and I could tell by the look in her eyes that she was going to do everything in her power to make sure I survived.

I knew that the three of them had me covered for however long I would have to be in Ottawa. For supper that night, Bonnie said she would make us a surprise (did I mention she's an amazing cook?) and showed up with homemade egg rolls. After dinner, we planned our strategy for getting to the hospital the next day and how we would pick up Bonnie along the way. The women sat together and wrote out questions for the doctors, then Bonnie headed home.

The next morning was D-Day. We headed out, stopped to pick up coffee, and then met Bonnie at the bus station. Dave and Bob dropped Sandra, Bonnie and me at the front door of the hospital and went to park the car. When we got into the hospital, Bonnie suggested a wheelchair, which was perfect because my energy level was low on a good day and she had mentioned it was a long walk.

Rather than look like I had been sucking back margaritas this early in the day, a wheelchair was a good idea. The hospital was a maze—long hallways going in every different direction, with little hallways leading off each of them. Sandra, Bonnie and I were in the lead. The guys were trailing behind us, looking like they were about to go for prostate exams. That didn't last long. We were nearing the appointment time, so when Bonnie put me in the wheelchair, she must have thought it was a road rally. I was looking for my seatbelt at one point and Sandra was doing everything in her power to keep up with us.

We found the wing of the hospital we were looking for, I registered, and my gang settled into the waiting room. We arrived looking like we had been travelling for days and now we were trying to find our five-star hotel. Instead, we had to settle for a pea-green hostel, chairs with vinyl that had seen way too much butt crack, and windows that didn't reach the top of the ceiling.

Dave and Bob looked like they would rather be any place but here. Honestly, they should have bars in hospitals. Why don't they? Get a couple shots of tequila, and then go in and get the shitty news. Ask the doc to write out the important details, go home in a cab. Read it later. Sounds like a good idea to me.

This is where it hit me and I started to laugh. I discovered this coping mechanism when I taught driving. Whenever a student would put me in a dangerous situation, I would laugh rather than yell. I realized that everyone around me looked really sick.

Shit, I'm here about a stem cell transplant. Wow, that's a fucking terrible colour to paint the walls. Definitely doesn't make me go to my happy place. Could the waiting area be any smaller? Might as well be a shipping container. Our immune systems are already in the crapper. Are they trying to make sure we all end up with a virus before we leave here? Oh, that's why they're handing out masks like there's a Lone Ranger convention going on.

Then my name was called. I took my posse with me, hoping the examination room was a little bigger than the waiting room. Wrong, definitely wrong. We looked like we were trying to get into a clown car. Who designs these rooms anyway? There must be a special hospital architect: "Yep, no bigger than a bathroom stall. That should be good."

I know the exam room isn't a hotel and the hospital isn't expecting Scotland Yard to show up with a patient, but you should have seen us. I was in a wheel-chair, Sandra was on the exam table, Bonnie was sitting in the lone chair, and the two guys were standing in whatever space was left. Enter the doc. I think we scared the shit out of him.

By way of introduction, I said: "This is my team."

He laughed, then introduced himself as Dr. Lamb. I explained how everyone was related to me and he explained that he was here to describe what would happen during the stem cell transplant.

Dr. Lamb started by saying that I would be receiving an allogeneic transplant, which meant that it would be coming from an unrelated donor. It was inconceivable to me to think that there was someone on the transplant list who could be a match for me.

The stem cell donor match doesn't have anything to do with your blood type, which I was ignorant about. Being B negative, which was a rare blood type, I was concerned about finding a match. I have since learned that certain ethnicities have a higher chance of having their stem cells matched. When it comes to other backgrounds, the numbers drop. There are specific criteria that matches a candidate with the needs of the patient. We definitely need more people on the registry.

Dr. Lamb went on to explain that there was a 15 to 25 per cent risk of infection. I asked if this was because of graft versus host disease, and he said yes.

Basically, when you receive a stem cell transplant, your body can accept the stem cells or reject them. If they accept them, it's called graft versus cancer. That means your body and mind happen to be in the right state to accept the cells, and the cells have decided to stay awhile.

If, on the other hand, these cells come in and your body says, "Who the fuck are you and what are you doing here?" You're in for a rough go, and that is called graft versus host disease. *You* being the host, of course.

It is the WWF of blood-disease fights.

That is why I had a picture in my mind of what the scene should look like after I had the transplant. It was going to have a koi-pond, Buddhist-retreat kind of look, yet with CIA qualities and a few margaritas thrown in once in a while. Make sense? I was trying to go with a calm happy place, yet with a few hidden cameras installed, in case any bad cells tried to act up. If that happened, I would try to calm them back down. I know that's something I couldn't do, but it was how my mind was working at the time.

Then Dr. Lamb said, "Chance of survival is 40 per cent."

My husband really didn't need to have that reiterated.

Again I'm thinking, *That's not happening.*

Besides, the odds were in my favour. A knock on the door and another doctor entered the room. He introduced himself as Dr. Doom. Right off the bat, he asked, "What are you doing in a wheelchair?"

"You tell me. I'm numb up to my armpits and my hemoglobin is in the 80's. That's not really a good combination for balance."

"What do you mean you're numb?"

"Just what I said. I have no feeling from my toes to my armpits, as well as the ends of my fingers."

He told me he had no idea what the cause could be, and that he had no idea the numbness was going on in the first place. I explained that I had told Dr. Sangfroid at the Sault Cancer Clinic a couple of times, and also to his coworker Dr. DeVain, the oncologist with whom I had my video conference. Both times I had been dismissed.

He then asked if I knew why I was here and I told him that Dr. Lamb had just explained the stem cell transplant procedure to us. Then for reasons unknown to all of us, he repeated it all over again. Exactly as Dr. Lamb had just finished telling us.

Oh, my God. Dr. Doom is Dr. Sangfroid's brother from another mother. Same bedside manner, not listening, autopilot bullshit. Did he not hear what I just said? I've already heard this. I let him finish, and then he and Dr. Lamb said they would be back in a couple of minutes.

On their return, Dr. Doom tried to explain to me that because of all the neuropathy and numbness I had been experiencing, the transplant could *not* take place. He would have to figure out what was going on first and that could take months.

Which is when I lost it.

"I've been told I have a year to a year and a half to live. That was February and now this is June. Now you're telling me I might have to wait until December? I don't think so."

"Oh, I wouldn't go by that timeline. Just go by how you're feeling."

How I'm feeling? How the fuck do you think I'm feeling? I look like the ghost of Christmas past, can't tell if I've pulled my pants up or not, and I'm in a wheelchair. Go by how I'm fucking feeling, you asshole. I'm number than a stump.

But I didn't say that.

He wanted me to see a specialist in neuropathy within the next two weeks before they proceeded with anything. I made sure I had everyone's phone numbers and told him I would hold him to the two-week timeframe.

We left the hospital after that. I think we were all in a state of shock. Bonnie had to return to work and the rest of us went for lunch. I had expected dates and answers, as I'm sure the rest of my friends did, and we were left with more questions. I was frustrated and disappointed. Also, I have to admit, a little scared. Especially if the doctors thought they were going to make me wait for a transplant.

The four of us talked about our next cruise together. We talked about what we were going to have for supper. Then I turned to them and said that I wanted to make team T-shirts for when I went in for the stem cell transplant. I wanted the name to be *Dragon(fly) Maidens* for the girls and *Dragon(fly) Warriors* for the guys, and underneath I wanted it to say, *Wasn't that a fucking ride!!* The rest of the way home we talked about colours and T-shirt styles, and everyone was excited. It made the ride go quickly.

When we returned to Sandra and Dave's, we all went for a nap. None of us felt like cooking, so we ordered a pizza, and Bonnie joined us for our last evening together before Bob and I returned to the Sault.

Before getting into bed that night I said to Bob, "There's something wrong. Something's missing."

So I started going through the prescriptions I took, but I'd already talked to the pharmacist and he knew that the three medications I was on didn't have the kind of neurological side effects that I was experiencing, and the local neurologist Dr. Gentil had agreed.

Then I started Googling the supplements I took every day. First, I started with vitamin C with B complex—no, it was fine. Next, fish oil. Nope, same thing. Calcium with vitamin D—yep, OK. Lastly, I looked at the zinc I had been taking, which was in 50 mg caplets. I had been taking two pills twice a day for the last five years. I queried the recommended dose and it was substantially less. I bolted upright in bed.

"There's not a lot of good things about zinc," I told my husband. "In fact, they're taking it out of denture adhesive and they're pulling some of the cold remedies off the market. I'm going to stop taking it."

CHAPTER 9

Zinc About It and Get Back To Me

THE WEEK AFTER WE RETURNED home from Ottawa, I was scheduled for blood work at the local cancer clinic. Keep in mind, I had stopped taking zinc on June 28 and my blood work was scheduled for July 2.

Nurse Merry, who always called on the same day with the results, said, " Hey, good news. Your hemoglobin is up!"

"To what?" I stammered. I was stunned.

"To 92."

"I went up six points?"

This meant I had fewer immature cells and a few more red blood cells (the ones that give us oxygen).

"Don't you think that's odd?" I asked.

"That's good news, no?"

"But MDS doesn't self-correct, and the only time my hemoglobin has gone up is when I've had a transfusion. Do you think it's because I stopped taking my zinc?"

"This is really bothering you, isn't it?

"Don't you think it should be?"

"Do you want me to ask Dr. Sangfroid?"

"I think that would be a good idea."

I thought I was starting to lose my mind.

She called back the next morning: "He says to tell you there's a five-point error margin in the lab."

"Good to know. So when I'm at 75, I could really be at 70 and actually need a transfusion. Someone is just blowing smoke up my ass and making me drag myself around for another two weeks until I can hardly stand up."

She actually chuckled a little. "Oh, never thought of that. Is there anything else?"

"No."

I sat there thinking, *WTF*. I must be certifiable. You start doubting yourself because *they* are the professionals. If the *doctor* says it's alright, I must be good to go. Yeah, for a dirt nap at the local cemetery.

Two days later I had a doctor's appointment with a specialist for an unrelated issue. I knew it would be quite a wait, so I went over to the office of another doctor I know. I would bend his ear once in a while when I had an appointment close by, and I knew I could count on him to answer some direct questions that had been eating away at me.

I had seen him in January after my first appointment with Dr. Sangfroid and he didn't recognize me because I had lost so much weight. Then I ran into him again during my husband's stay at the hospital after his nosebleed.

"You still look good," he said to me then, ever the quick wit.

"You didn't fucking recognize me," I replied. "What are you talking about? I look like I'm anorexic."

Even that day in March I was pissed off at some other doctor and he let me vent and was laughing hysterically when I left.

We talk the same talk.

So, when I went into his office in an emotional upheaval, he took the time to talk to me.

First thing out of his mouth was, "Why don't you have a fucking cane?"

I must have looked stunned for a minute.

"Funny, I was thinking I should be using one. How come no one else has told me to use one?"

"They are all fucking assholes."

We laughed. I went on to tell him that I seriously thought people were going to call the police on us when my husband and I were leaving restaurants because I was stumbling so badly. We discussed a little more about the numbness, which I thought hadn't been taken seriously enough, and what he thought about it.

On the way out of the office, he handed me a little piece of paper.

"What's this?"

"It's a two-for-one hip replacement, which you are going to need if you don't get a cane. You probably need all that shit for the bathroom too, am I right?"

I laughed, nodding. I thanked him for taking the time to talk to me, gave him a hug and left. I went to the medical supply store right away and did as he said. Funny, I often thought it perplexing that no one else noticed I looked like a weeble, one of those roly-poly children's dolls with a round base that rolls and sways from side to side.

As I left the doctor's office that day, the transplant unit called to say they had a potential match. I can't even begin to explain the feeling of relief that gave me. During the drive home, I was planning a way to make sure the doctors would figure out what was going on with me so I could have the transplant.

A week later I'm back in Ottawa to see a few more specialists, but more importantly, to see a neurologist. Not any neurologist. This is Dr. Power. I think I liked her right from the start because she talks like my other doctor friend who suggested I get a cane. Frankly, she just talks like me. She is an amazing doctor, brilliant and funny, but best of all, very direct.

My condition seemed to be of the utmost fascination to her, and I made it quite clear to her that it was her blessing I needed before I would be allowed to proceed with the bone marrow transplant. She put me through a couple of "fun tests" to see how my nerve endings were reacting, and then met up with Sandra and me in her office.

"You realize the chemo from the stem cell transplant can actually cripple you. The hemotologists won't tell you that."

I liked her even more for telling me the truth.

"Well, better crippled than dead."

It's funny. All of the hemotologists were kind of like, *Ooh, what's going on with you? Can't touch that. Come back and see me when you're better.*

Dr. Power never treated me that way. She was always respectful and looked me in the eye when she talked to me.

Then there was Dr. Gray. I had an appointment with Dr. Gray after Dr. Power one day and I took Bonnie with me. Nothing against young doctors, but if they have no life skills or palliative experience, I find it hard for them to look you in the eye.

We went into the exam room and I have now learned to ask this question first when I meet a new doctor: "What is your specialty?"

"I'm a hematologist," she replied.

OMG, hematologists are all cut from the same cloth. Dr. Gray had a nondescript haircut and a soft-spoken voice, and oh, did I mention she looked like she had just graduated? Maybe she hadn't, but that was my impression. I could feel my heart starting to race.

"Why am I dealing with another hematologist? By the way, how many doctors are on my team?"

"Well, actually 12 different doctors," she said in a sweet voice.

"Why can't I meet them all at once?"

"Oh, that would be too difficult."

"OK, what do you want to talk about?"

"I wanted to talk to you about Vidaza."

"CHEMO!" I almost screamed. My blood pressure must have went through the roof, but I tried to maintain my composure.

"You want to talk to me about chemo? I don't fucking think so. Why in the world would you want to give it to me now?"

She literally started waving her hand up and down in front of me like she was Cinderella's fairy godmother and said, "Well, we don't know what's going on with you."

"So you think chemo will make it better? Who's idea was this? Chemo is not discriminate. It's not going to go in there and say, 'Hey, are you in the MDS gang? We want you out!' No, absolutely not. I'm healthy. I haven't lost any more weight and I haven't had a cold or the flu. Besides, I'll be back in two weeks for the stem cell and that chemo will be bad enough."

At this point Bonnie stepped in and said, "You're telling Karen this is a back-up plan?"

"This better be a back-up to a fucking back-up plan," I answered.

Dr. Gray was getting more and more flustered. Finally, she spoke: "OK, well, we'll just wait to see what happens."

"Good idea."

Who comes up with this stuff? Do the doctors sit around the table and toss around ideas? *Oh yeah, that Zachary woman. Still don't know what's causing the numbness. Any ideas? I got nothing. You got anything? Nope. Oh, I know. Chemo.*

Really!

I couldn't figure out why the doctors would want to give me chemo now. I had been staying as healthy as I could, keeping away from people who were sick and places where there were lots of people around. I washed my hands religiously and was eating as well as could be expected. I knew that the stem cell transplant only had a 40 per cent survival rate. Why would I want to risk my immune system getting weaker before then? Weren't these doctors asking the same questions?

Now for the *pièce de résistance*. (You're not going to believe this.)

Two days after my appointment with Dr. Gray, I had to meet with Dr. Doom. You'll remember him from my earlier appointment at the transplant unit in Ottawa at the end of June. He was with Dr. Lamb and reiterated the whole stem cell procedure and then told me I wasn't going to have it. (I'm still sure Dr. Doom's related to Dr. Sangfroid, the hematologist in the Sault.)

He entered the exam room and told me that Dr. Power, the neurologist, had cleared me for the stem cell transplant. Seeing as how we had a donor, I was ready for the procedure.

Once again, he went over the details.

"Can I ask you a question?"

"Sure."

"What was my hemoglobin on Wednesday?"

I was curious, as I had stopped taking the zinc a couple of weeks before and my hemoglobin (the oxygen cells) had climbed. Now I wanted to know if there were any more changes.

He flipped through my chart: "96."

"Wow, I've gone up 10 points since I stopped taking my zinc."

"Mrs. Zachary, are you trying to tell me you don't think you have MDS?"

"Well, I don't know what I'm trying to tell you, but don't you think it's odd that my hemoglobin is up

10 points in a couple of weeks since I stopped taking zinc?"

"Mrs. Zachary, you have MDS and you'll be back here in two weeks for a stem cell, so go home and get your affairs in order and we'll see you back soon."

So that's what I did. I went home, I started organizing my clothing and shoes, and had lunch with my friends.

CHAPTER 10

Penny For Your Thoughts...

At the February appointment with Doctor Sangfroid in the Sault, I had asked him about a Dr. Sage, whom I had heard about in Ottawa. Friends of mine had told me he had saved their daughter's life.

Doctor Sangfroid's head snapped up and he said to me sarcastically: "You won't ever get to meet him. He's basically retired."

It was like his tone implied "What were you thinking?" Like I was trying to get a hold of God.

"Oh, OK."

When I was getting into the shower the last Friday in July, I handed my cell phone to my husband and said, "You have to answer this if it rings. It's the main number the Ottawa transplant unit has for me. You just have to look after it until I get out of the shower."

He literally hates the phone, particularly cell phones, and almost never checks messages.

"Alright," he finally said begrudgingly.

First thing out of the shower: "Who called?"

I knew the phone had rung because I left the door propped open.

"Some doctor," he replied.

I could have screamed. "You're kidding, right? What was his name?"

"I don't know."

"Did you write it down?"

So I started listing off all of the doctors: Dr. Doom, Dr. Lamb, Dr. DeVain, Dr. Power. Nope.

Then he finally says, "He said to tell you to bring your bottles of zinc and he thinks you have a copper deficiency."

I remember a chill running through me, but I was on my way to lunch with my mom and all I could think was, *They've found a way to get rid of the numbness and pain, and I won't be crippled after the transplant.*

During lunch with my mother the phone started ringing regarding appointments, and the Bone

Marrow Transplant unit wanted me there quickly. This was a Friday, the end of July, and they wanted me there on Monday for a new ECG, because (oops, forgot to tell you) the last one was really bad. My heart wasn't working up to capacity. I asked the assistant in the BMT unit which doctor had called and she said Dr. Sage.

"I thought he was retired," I said, a bit confused.

"Oh no, he still does some work here."

I look back on it now and realize how many things I didn't know. Now that I've had some time to reflect, I don't believe that one of the doctors finally said, "By Jove, I believe I've got it, and I don't think we're going down the right path."

What I do believe, and this is *my* belief, is that *all* of the results had finally come back from the blood work Dr. Gentil, my neurologist in the Sault, had sent me for in June. I believe with all my heart that Dr. Gentil did everything in his power, including faxing the results of the blood work and circling the zinc and copper levels, to the Ottawa Hospital.

One thing I do know for sure is that afternoon when I returned from lunch after Dr. Sage first called, I looked up information about copper deficiency.

Then I looked straight at my husband and said, "I don't think I have cancer. I think somebody fucked up. All of these symptoms about copper deficiency describe exactly what's going on with me."

Sunday I left for Ottawa.

On Monday I completed a nuclear stress test, which is where they inject you with a stimulant to simulate the treadmill exercise. They must have figured out my numbness and co-ordination were so bad that if the tech cranked up the treadmill too much I would have looked like a kite in the wind.

They also took an echocardiogram to see how well my heart was working, followed by blood work on Wednesday. I had my first meeting with Dr. Sage the next morning. Along for the ride was my sidekick and best friend, Sandra.

Sandra and I waited in our now favourite exam room, where we tried desperately not to take out Sharpies and write our names somewhere. Those walls were desperately in need of decorating. Also, we had been in this room a few times, so we thought we were allowed that much.

The doctor came in and introduced himself to us. Dr. Sage is a distinguished older doctor, white hair and moustache, a bit reserved, but he has a twinkle in his eye. I knew my bluntness made him wince a few times. He struck me as a gentleman, kind but direct. I liked him.

I handed him the bag that contained my zinc pills. He pulled them out and looked at them, then asked, "Why did you start taking these?"

"Well, around five years ago, I had been watching someone I thought was a well-respected doctor on television, and he was touting zinc as an immune booster. Seeing as I was a customs inspector and out in the cold a lot, and I was handling documents and dealing with the travelling public, I thought these could help keep me healthy."

He looked the pills over once again and looked back at me. "You have a copper deficiency."

He described how the zinc I was taking had caused the numbness because the copper and zinc were at such an imbalance and had been for quite a while. He went on to tell me that he was waiting for a few more test results, but in the interim, he was putting the transplant on hold. I asked him if I understood correctly that I didn't have cancer.

"I want to have all the results first, so I'll see you on Monday."

In both my head and in my heart, I knew it wasn't cancer. Still, you want to hear it from the doctor.

My son, Josh, and his girlfriend, Lise, had arrived in Ottawa over the weekend. They stayed with me at Bonnie's, and on Monday they accompanied Sandra and me to the hospital for the final diagnosis.

It was a strange feeling, sitting in the exam room and thinking that I was going to be told that I *didn't* have cancer when I was supposed to be back for a transplant soon.

We all rammed into that small room again and waited for Dr. Sage. He arrived a few minutes later, and I introduced him to Josh and Lise.

He got right to the point and said, "You don't have cancer."

I must have looked pretty stunned because he said, "Well, you don't look very happy for someone I just told she doesn't have cancer."

"You didn't magically tap me on the head and make me all better. I'm sorry if I seem ungrateful, but I shouldn't be like this. No one listened to me. I'm in constant pain. I need a walker and a cane. I get it, trust me, I know how lucky I am that I'm not going to die, but seriously, how did this happen? How many other people has this happened to already?"

"Well, you're not your brother's keeper, Karen. You should only worry about yourself."

"You know, when I checked into the cancer clinic in the Sault, they have you fill out a 12-page document. Probably the same here. Why bother? Everything was on it. Where I was in pain, the vitamins I was taking, and then the nurse comes in and asks me the same questions all over again. I don't get it. I want this fixed."

Dr. Sage explained that he had never dealt with a case like mine before, but he would do some research and see what he could do.

I asked about another bone marrow biopsy because I wanted to ensure I didn't have cancer, and he said he would schedule one.

A couple of days later I returned to the hospital and he did the biopsy himself. He told me that he had discovered that copper deficiency was rare, and I was one of 35 cases in the world. Even more rare was the fact that the copper deficiency had disguised itself as myelodysplastic syndrome.

I went on to tell him that my dog Theo has a copper storage disease.

He looked at me and said, "Oh, Wilson's disease. Wow, that's synchronicity."

We talked at length about how this could be prevented in the future. I told him I understood how frustrating it must be for doctors to stay on top of the prescription drugs people were taking, let alone vitamins and other herbal supplements. We talked about other ways to deal with this kind of problem, such as creating a database with the recommended daily amounts for vitamins that could convey to the doctor when the patient was over the limit.

I flew home that night both physically and emotionally exhausted.

The next month I had an appointment with both Dr. Sage and the pharmacist, Henry Houdini. I would be the first Ottawa Hospital patient ever treated with a copper deficiency and they had decided on six intravenous copper infusions. I was to arrive at the Bone Marrow Transplant unit the next morning for the first dose, and Dr. Sage would have someone call on the weekend to set up the rest.

Early the next morning, I arrived at the unit and was introduced to the nurse who would be looking after me. Her name was Penny.

At first it didn't click, but then one of the staff said, "Hey, it's pretty funny that you're giving her the copper, eh, Penny?"

CHAPTER 11

The New Civil Engineer Needs Rosetta Stone

I RECEIVED A CALL FROM the Ottawa Hospital to see Dr. Power for a new EMG and to meet with Dr. Sage regarding the treatments for the copper deficiency. I couldn't wait.

For months my balance had declined and the pain in my nerve endings was becoming intolerable. The numbness had spread almost to my shoulders and extended to my limbs. My hands were a real problem, especially the ends of my fingers. I had asked my GP, Dr. Kevin, about physiotherapy and he thought it was a good idea.

The first physiotherapist I went to put me on a treadmill. I was thinking to myself, *Are you fucking kidding me? I can't feel the ground when it's not moving, and you're going to put me on ground that is moving? Is this a reality show?*

Never went back.

At the appointment in Ottawa, Dr. Power agreed that physio would be good but couldn't believe that a PT would put me on a treadmill after I had explained my neurological issues to him.

At the end of the EMG, she said I had improved somewhat, not enough that I would notice, but enough that the machine would pick it up. She was shocked to hear the final diagnosis had been copper deficiency, and then went on to tell me that she has had patients over the years who look like they have ALS, or Lou Gehrig's Disease, when in actuality it was a vitamin E deficiency.

We agreed that I would come back every six months because I would need to be under neurological care more that hematology.

For people who know me, they would say I'm independent and like to take control of situations, so when I flew back to Ottawa for the copper treatments, I decided to rent a car. I felt that I had been enough of a burden on Sandra, Dave and Bonnie.

How hard could driving back and forth from the hospital be, right? If anything, the copper treatments will make me feel better instantly, wouldn't they? I didn't get the car until Sunday, and at first the rental place gave me a truck, but I returned it and picked up a Fiat 500.

The interesting thing was that Sandra and I had been talking all weekend about how similar we were in our walking and our movements. Sandra had been diagnosed with multiple sclerosis in her early 40's, and her symptoms included tingling, pins and needles, numbness, muscle weakness, and difficulties in coordination and balance.

"You know you can remap your brain," she said.

"What do you mean?"

"Well, if you've had an illness or injury that caused you to stop doing a movement in a certain way, you can retrain your brain to do it another way."

Interesting. Never thought about it like that.

It felt like all the highways and back roads I had been using before my illness were suddenly wiped out, and the landscape all around was destroyed by forest fires. Gone was my instinct to keep walking and trust that I knew what I was doing. Gone was the sense that I could close my eyes in the shower and not topple over and land face first in the bathtub. Gone was the trust between my brain and my feet. My brain was now asking me to look at my feet at all times to ensure they knew what they were doing.

So I started to pretend I had a new civil engineer in my brain. The Old Guy had been killed by too much zinc and my brain was fighting with human resources to get another one. I finally decided on the New Guy. The only problem was that he didn't speak the language of Karen.

I started laying out all the new road ideas that I would like to have. Then I thought, *I think the new civil engineer needs Rosetta Stone.* I ordered it for him; it just took a while for it to arrive.

That was the scene on the second day of my copper infusions. I hadn't been driving very much, but I had already been to one appointment and back. I started to think that the remapping was really working.

It was a beautiful day. Three o'clock in the afternoon. Cute Fiat 500. No one around. Parking gate. Numb foot.

I arrived at the gate and I'm on my Bluetooth headset, talking to Bonnie about the appointment. I pulled up to the card read, stopped, reached for the parking card, and suddenly my foot slipped off the brake. It was jammed on the gas and I couldn't get it off.

Vrooommm! Boing! The gate bounced off the windshield and I tore out of the gate, still nobody around, and I was screaming. I glanced in the rear-view mirror and the gate was dangling by a thread.

By this time I could hear Bonnie screaming in my ear, "Karen, what's the matter. What's wrong?"

Now there's a stop sign coming up, but I can't go straight because there's a cement curb about a foot high and I'd shear the tires off this little fucker, so I cranked the wheels and all you could hear was *screeeeeeeccchhhh!*

Finally, I hit the brake. Still no one was around. I was sobbing. I could hear Bonnie's voice again, "Karen, what happened?"

"I *jjjusst hhit* a *pparking* gate." *Sniff, sniff.*

"Just leave. Nobody will know," she said.

"How does that work? When I return the car to the rental office, they'll ask, 'Is there anything you want to tell us, Mrs. Zachary? Say, maybe about a parking gate at the hospital?'

'Nope, wasn't me. Someone must have used it while I was in the hospital. What are you, nuts? I gotta go.' "

I got out of the car and I swear on a stack of Bibles, *not a scratch*. Then I called Sandra, because that's where I was going for supper that night. I was blubbering when she answered the phone and asked what's wrong.

She said the same thing as Bonnie: "Just leave."

"What is it with you Ottawa people? Just leave? I'll call you back later."

So I called Bob.

"What's wrong?"

I could hardly talk.

"Karen, stop crying. Are you hurt?"

"No."

"Is anyone else hurt?"

"No."

"You're absolutely right. Go and tell security what happened. I know you. You won't be able to live with yourself if you don't."

Away I went, parked at the front and went inside, didn't even take my cane, which in hindsight was *not* a good choice.

A young female surgeon (everyone looked like they were 16 years old that day) came out of a room still in her mask and gown, and said to me, "Are you alright?"

"Oh yeah, sure. Can you tell me which way to security?"

I probably looked like the drunk ghost of Christmas past. I arrived at security, my heart pounding, sweating like I had just run a marathon, and the young (*younnng!*) man behind the counter asked, "Can I help you?"

"Yes, my foot slipped off the brake and I bent the parking gate. I wanted to know what you wanted me to do."

He looked at me, unconcerned. "Oh, that happens all the time!

I felt like someone had hit the back of my knees.

"Really?" I said incredulously.

"Oh yeah."

He proceeded to grab a scrap of paper and asked for my name and address. If that didn't calm me down enough, a second female security officer just as young came flying into the doorway.

"Is she in the parking garage?"

"No, parking gate," he replied.

She waved her hand in a dismissive fashion, like she had bigger problems.

I returned the rental the next day, and I didn't drive again for eight months. After supper at Sandra's house that night, we were sitting on the deck having a drink and she gently pointed out to me that I had taken on too much, that I shouldn't have discounted how much those treatments had taken out of me mentally as well as physically.

Just like the blood transfusions, I thought by the second copper treatment I would feel an explosive amount of energy and well-being. Again, that wasn't the case.

The new civil engineer and I have had several conversations since then and he's starting to learn the new language. We are starting to heal together.

CHAPTER 12

Accepting Apologies

I HAD BALLOONS WITH ME when I came home from Ottawa. Not nice *Get Well Soon* balloons with happy faces on them. Big anger balloons, enough to take me on a ride for a few months.

I was mad at myself for what had happened with the car. I was mad because my family was supposed to be getting my psychic messages as to what to do for me and what not to do for me. Even some of the friends I had expected to hear from I still haven't talked to.

My friends who *were* there for me took me out for lunch and to the movies, dropped me off at appointments, or just stopped in for a visit.

Wouldn't you think someone in the medical profession would've suggested counselling? Hello? You have a year and a half to live. Did we tell you that?

Sorry, we were just kidding. What do you mean, you can't walk, or ride your motorcycle, or probably shouldn't be driving a car? Really?!?

My anger must have been palpable because at a birthday gathering a family member suggested a name for a counsellor. She said she'd known someone who had spoken to Liz and liked her. I called the next day. Liz is a wonderful counsellor. I had never had therapy and probably should have done so years ago after some problems at work. But that's a whole other book.

She was patient, kind, understanding and knew how to place me gently back on the rails after I had careened off them. For the *first* time someone acknowledged what I had been through and that I was still going through a terrible loss. I needed to start healing, and in order to do that, I had to look after myself. Not something I'm used to. I'm a "fixer." I want to look after everyone else's problems, and that was significantly (and still is, to a degree) slowing down my healing process.

I learned that "spinning" isn't just for bikes. It's an internal turmoil that feels like it starts in my stomach and goes right to my head, my mouth opens and out comes verbal diarrhea. I've had to learn to control what that kind of feeling does to me. But to be honest, a lot of things make me feel that way.

One day Liz asked, "Why aren't you more direct with people about what's bothering you?"

"Well, because it usually comes out sounding like I've slapped them."

"You just have to be kind, true, and necessary," she said sweetly.

"Ahh, that would be the problem. I always think what I have to say is *necessary*. It just never comes out kind and true."

She laughed.

Not only was the counselling helpful, but I had found a great physiotherapist. He was referred to me by the doctor who suggested I needed a cane. He had given me three names.

"You'll probably have to wait for the first two, and I know how patient you are." He laughed. "Better go with John."

I couldn't ask for someone who understood my situation better. The exercises he suggested helped my new civil engineer get through Chapter 1 of *The Language of Karen* right off the bat. Which made it possible to stop walking like I had shit my pants. I could now recognize the sensation that my legs were not being fully extended. I had been walking with them bent for months.

When I came home from physio one day, there was the familiar letter from the cancer clinic that I had seen multiple times over the last few months. This time it wasn't requesting blood work or diagnostic tests, but an appointment to see Dr. Sangfroid.

I went from zero to *are you fucking kidding me?* I hadn't seen him in seven months. What did he want with me? Well, I sure knew what I wanted with him. I still had quite a few anger balloons holding me up, and man, was I spinning. Could've started a fire. But I thought, *What the hell? I want to see what he has to say after all this time. I'll make the appointment.* And I did.

Then I called my counsellor. She suggested I come to see her the day before the appointment, so we could, you know, get some questions laid out, think about how I was going to ask them, and let me get out of there with some dignity.

Dignity? I thought. *I'm going to leave him with a new asshole.*

"Trust me, Karen. You won't get rid of the anger that way."

"Really? You're sure about that?"

"Yes."

If she wasn't so fucking calm all the time, I'd probably argue more. But she stopped my spinning very quickly.

On the day of the appointment, Bob went to the hospital with me. We made our way to the cancer clinic to meet Dr. Sangfroid. When I got to the counter to register, the nurse asked me to keep my health card out because I'd have to fill out those long, drawn-out forms. I could feel the anxiety and the spinning start. It's like a blood pressure spike and my stomach started churning.

Instead, as calmly as I could, I looked at her and said, "I'm not filling out any form."

"Well, the nurse will need it."

"She can ask me why I didn't fill it out."

"Well, OK."

I sat down in one of the chairs and waited for Bob, who had gone to park the car. When he came in, I just about exploded and said, "Can you believe they wanted me to fill out those forms? They didn't even look at the last one."

"Calm down, Karen."

They called us into the exam room, and soon after Nurse Merry walked in. Her green eyes looked like they never closed.

"How are you?" she asked in a high-pitched voice.

"Not great."

How the fuck do you think I am?

Sometimes she's way too happy for me, and today was one of those days.

"You didn't fill in the form for us."

"No, I didn't. No one read the last one or we wouldn't be in this mess."

"Oh, OK."

"Why am I here?"

"Dr. Sangfroid just wanted to do a follow-up. Can I get you on the scale for your weight?"

"Fine." She took my blood pressure and my temperature, and asked some basic questions. She could tell I wasn't happy about being there.

"Dr. Sangfroid will be right in."

Bob and I sat waiting, and I tried to remain calm. When Dr. Sangfroid arrived, the first thing he asked was how I was doing.

"Not great." I wasn't in the mood for chitchat. "Why am I here, Dr. Sangfroid? Why did you want to see me?"

"I'm supposed to keep an eye on your blood levels, if you still want me to."

"We'll see how this goes first. I have some questions."

1. Did you know I told Nurse Merry I went off zinc when she called me regarding the blood work on July 2?
2. Did you get a copy of the blood work from Dr. Gentil in June regarding my zinc and copper levels?
3. Why didn't you call me back and investigate when my hemo went up six points?
4. Do you have the genetic testing report for monosomy 7? I'd like a copy of it.

Basically, questions 1 and 3 were answered the same way, that there's a five-point error margin in the lab. The answer was *no* to questions 2 and 4. Monosomy 7, a genetic marker occasionally found in patients with MDS and acute leukemia, had been discovered in my first bone marrow biopsy.

"I am so disappointed in how you handled my trust in you, especially when I kept asking about the numbness in the ends of my fingers and toes."

"I'm not a neurologist, Karen."

"Exactly. Why didn't you refer me to one?"

"Yes, I should have."

"I want you to go forward paying attention to your patients and the questions they have, *not* dismissing them."

"I'll try," he said.

At this point, I was still looking for those two words I needed to hear. But I figured, *Oh well, at least I said what I needed to say.* I got off the table and Dr. Sangfroid headed to the door. He shook my husband's hand and looked at me.

"I don't suppose you want a handshake?"

"Actually, I want a hug."

So I grabbed him and hugged him tight, and he said to me quietly, "I'm so sorry, Karen."

All my balloons popped at once.

CHAPTER 13

Exit 101

ON THE WAY HOME FROM the hospital that day, Bob said
to me, "We're really lucky we don't have to go back to
the cancer clinic."

Dr. Sangfroid told me that our next appointment
would be in the ambulatory care section because I
would no longer be considered urgent care. It was at
this point that I realized how much the trips to the
cancer clinic had drained my husband.

"Yes, it is, and we didn't even see the inside of the
chemo suite, so we should be very grateful for that."

Then Bob started talking about the fact that Dr.
Sangfroid had asked to continue seeing me and I had
agreed. I wanted to see if he really was going to be a
better doctor.

Now that I was starting to heal and people were starting to find out I wasn't dying, it was interesting and sometimes disturbing to see their reactions. I would run into people who had heard about my misdiagnosis and they would ask me what happened.

At the beginning, I didn't have it all figured out in my head yet either, and when I told people it was a copper deficiency, some people felt the information I gave them was enough and left it at that.

But others would push. Some would push more. The really toxic ones made me feel like I'd tried to commit a slow suicide over five years.

They would say, "I hear you were suffering from a zinc overdose. What amount were you taking? Why were you taking so much?"

And I would say, "No, it was a zinc accumulation that caused a copper deficiency and I didn't understand how the body processes metals."

I was embarrassed answering these questions. I had wanted to stay healthy and damn near died trying. Looking back, I was so exhausted that I didn't know how to stand up for myself. Foolishly, I felt I owed everyone an explanation.

If a life sentence hadn't been attached to the cancer I'd originally been diagnosed with, I'm not so sure I would've felt the need to explain what happened to me. How do you tell people that you're dying and now you're not when you don't even understand it yourself?

My counsellor said, "Depending on who you're talking to, you can look at it as a newspaper article. You have the headline, the paragraph, or the whole article. You decide who gets what."

Sounded like a good plan, but for the most part, people (not all) couldn't get past the zinc part of the story or the fact that I didn't have cancer.

Well, you must be just fine now, right? Are you going back to work? You must be so happy, eh?

Some days I thought I had switched languages or I had had a stroke while I was talking. Maybe my civil engineer had gone on strike or hadn't gotten to the right chapter in the Rosetta Stone.

Some people wanted to jump to their own conclusions. Sometimes my husband would just walk away; he was so tired of hearing about it, and if we went out for dinner with another couple and we ran into someone we knew, I could see his face change. That look of "Oh, no, here we go again."

Slowly, it started to get a bit better, but now people would come up to me and say, "Hey, you look great."

Which I know sounds funny. Why would I be angry about a comment like that? But looks are deceiving when it comes to neurological issues and other serious illnesses. I was still in constant pain every day, and the numbness made my balance a challenge. I stopped driving for eight months, which was frustrating. On the upside, physiotherapy helped to remap my brain. I had put the weight back on that I had lost, and my hemoglobin was back up, so my colour was good.

I knew why people were saying that I looked good, but mentally I was screaming, *Stop saying that!*

I knew I'd had enough when I went to see Dr. Gentil, my very nice neurologist. He walked in and the first thing he said to me was, "Wow, you look great."

I could feel the spin cycle kick in instantly.

Instead, I stayed calm. "Dr. Gentil, I don't mean this in a bad way, but I swear to God, if one more person says that to me, I'm going to hit them over the head with my cane. Which actually won't do much good because it folds in three places!"

He looked a little stunned.

I continued. "Everyone keeps saying that I look great, but I feel like shit. I want to crawl out of my skin. I get it, I look in the mirror, I try to do my best to not look like I'm heading for a dirt nap. But seriously!"

"I know, Karen. No one can understand the amount of pain you're in."

Pop! All those balloons popped again. I felt bad. I started to cry.

"We will work on a plan to get this pain under control."

He was true to his word, and within a month, I had the pain to a tolerable level. Dr. Gentil is the kind of doctor who should be a role model for others.

With my pain under control, I went back to the counsellor with another problem. I explained that I was still having problems with toxic people.

I had recently been to a family event and a woman I had never met came over and introduced herself, explaining that a relative had told her what had happened. She was a retired nurse and she wanted to know all about it. Except she did all the talking. I thought I knew what was coming, but I didn't have any idea. It was like being assaulted. I told Bob to go out for a smoke.

It was like having several bandages ripped off open wounds very slowly over and over again. Oddly enough, this had happened to me a few months before by another retired nurse.

"Why didn't you say something?" the counsellor asked.

"I tried, but she knew everything, and I just froze. That's never happened."

"You need an exit plan."

"What do you mean by that?"

"Well, for the first little while, like two weeks, you can lie and say, 'I can't talk right now, gotta be somewhere,' or something like that. Next step, in the next few months, something a little more vague like, 'Can I get back to you,' knowing you won't. And the last step is just saying, 'This has been really hard on me and I'd really not like to talk about it.' "

When I came home that day, I talked to Bob about what Liz had told me, and he said, "I think you should go straight to Plan C."

I replied, "Oh, and she also said you should help me get out of these situations, as opposed to the stop, drop, and roll."

He agreed. He said when he runs into people and they ask how I am, he says I'm fine.

"Perfect," I said. "That's what I'm saying too. I'm good."

Some people got caught off-guard when they saw me. They'd hear the stories about me almost dying, and now that I wasn't, they couldn't comprehend the physical disabilities I was still faced with. I have talked to a few friends who have had similar physical limitations after chemo.

In my experience, many people struggling with health issues don't want to hear "You look good." What that means to the patient is, "You looked like shit the last time I saw you."

It might be better to say something like, "Nice to see you" or "I'm so happy to see you." That way, you're not commenting on their physical appearance or giving them the third degree.

Now when people ask how I'm doing, I say I'm fine, because I am, for the most part. I know how fortunate I am to be a throwback, to have been caught, then told, "Oh her? Nope. Not her. We have enough problems, thanks. You can throw her back in the water."

CHAPTER 14

The Gravel Road

IF YOU SURVEYED PEOPLE AND asked them: If you were taking a long trip, which road would you prefer to travel on, a highway or a gravel road?

The majority of people would probably say, "The highway, of course."

Why not? It's smoother, usually safer, straighter, you're not eating dust, and you can get on and off as you please thanks to the exits.

If you're a motorcyclist, you find out very quickly that Jan the GPS lady can't find most gravel roads. You take a quick glance at the screen only to find that she's put you in the middle of a field or a desert or a lake. Suddenly, you're screaming at the machine: "Where the fuck am I, Jan? Could you do this a little quicker? The road's about to end."

I was on a day trip on my motorcycle with my girlfriend Maria a couple of years back. Maria is an amazing person and a skilled motorcyclist. We had been on several trips together, including two to Tennessee.

On this particular beautiful day, we stopped for lunch, and realizing we had time to spare going home, decided to take a little detour. There's a back road we both love full of S curves that would take us to the little town just east of the Sault where Maria lived.

We had our wireless headsets on and were talking about how the traffic was nice and light, and how good it felt to be on our bikes. I was the lead bike for the trip home. We turned onto a back highway and crossed a set of railroad tracks, and I saw a sign for construction ahead. All of a sudden I felt an icy chill run down my back.

"Maria, is there construction on this road?"

Not that Maria cared. She could ride through a hurricane.

"I don't know, Bella," she said in a singsong voice. Why?"

"Didn't you see the sign?"

"Well, I don't drive back here all the time just because I live around here. Don't worry, we'll be fine."

I know this is going to sound funny, but I'd had the bike a few years by then, and had only ridden a handful of times on gravel. Well, that day it was trial by fire. The next curve we came around, there it was: gravel. And not just any kind of gravel. The kind of gravel that's like loon shit. It felt like you were driving in sand. The tires would sink into the road, and you had to plow through and make your own lane.

"Maria! What the fuck!"

She started laughing.

"This isn't funny!"

"Just keep going. You'll be fine."

And I was, sweating like a steer, cursing up a storm, my mind in overdrive. Then we were back on pavement. For about 10 seconds, but long enough to look back and see Maria. She looked like a swamp monster. I was covering her in dust and she wasn't saying a word. In fact, she was enjoying it.

"Look, it says there's more construction. Do you want to get off?" she asked me.

"No, I know I can do it now. Screw it. Let's go."

The next part wasn't even half as bad, but the best thing for me was knowing I could do it. By the time we arrived at the intersection to part ways, she was white as a ghost, and we stopped for a second, soaking wet, to have a laugh.

I often thought of that day as the months went by during my illness. My misdiagnosis had been empowering in the same way. When I was first diagnosed, I didn't realize I had a choice with any of my health care needs until my doctor told me I could get a second opinion. All of a sudden, I went from starting chemo to getting a stem cell transplant.

At first you think, *God, they've given me a year to live.* Then you have to figure out if it's going to be fight or flight.

Meeting your problems head on doesn't mean you're disrespecting the doctor; it means you are looking after yourself. I have had so many people tell me that they or their family members would have taken the chemotherapy. Why? I fully understand if it's the last thing to try, but most of the people I talked to hadn't even considered a second opinion. Especially people older than me. Yet they wouldn't buy the first car they test drove.

The last time I saw Dr. Sage in Ottawa, when he told me that I was not my brother's keeper, I had already made up my mind to write a book, and I told him so. I think at first he thought I was joking.

It was no surprise to me when, a few weeks later, he called to tell me that the second bone marrow biopsy results, which had been missing, were located, and that I no longer had the monosomy 7 genetic marker. I still don't know if I ever had monosomy 7 or if the first test results were inconclusive.

He went on to tell me that copper deficiency was extremely rare and he decided to write a paper about me. If even one doctor read the paper, maybe it would help.

I felt like I was on pavement again, and the little GPS motorcycle wasn't driving in the middle of a field anymore. I was going to call my mom and tell her I was going to have a drink, but I had a cup of tea and enjoyed some time to myself instead.

I'm very slowly starting to heal, both physically and emotionally. It will be a gravel road for a while, but I'm OK with that.

Epilogue

MY COUNSELLOR DIDN'T WANT ME to write this book because she felt that I was just starting to heal and it wouldn't be a healthy experience for me. I'm not going to tell you it was easy reliving certain parts, but ultimately it has made me stronger.

I know what I am capable of now and it is much more than I thought it would be. I struggled with so many changes in my life, including physical limitations. Some days it felt overwhelming and I thought I would never feel like myself again.

My friend Dale is a quadriplegic and he helped me to see that I had set my own limitations. He taught me you can do anything if you set your mind to it, and you can do it with humour and dignity.

That's probably why I hate the word *no*. It's uncompromising, unyielding, there is no give. When you are dealing with a trauma or are recovering from one, it's one word you definitely do not want to hear.

So don't give in. Get what you want. It's your life. Ride it like you stole it!

Thank you to my family and friends

To my husband, Bob, who loves me more.

To my son, Josh, whom I still believe is too good to be mine. You are respectful, kind, loving and honest. Thank you for being there when I needed someone to listen. I love you so much.

To Sandra and Dave, for their unconditional love, hell-raising rides and comfort food.

To my dear friend Bonnie, who cared for me, protected me, fed me jelly beans, but most of all, believed I would survive.

To my mom and my brother, for your love and support. I love you both.

Shirin, to the wisest and most beautiful woman I have ever met. Thank you for taking good care of me. Love you too, baby.

To Kellie, you always seem to know when I need to talk, and your kind, wise words helped me through the worst. Sags rock.

Michele: "Sister," you've always known the right things to say and the right cards to send. You've always made me feel like family, and that in itself was healing.

To Donnie and Kelly, for your friendship and support, not to mention looking after my "baby" for me.

Candice and Fred, thank you for being there not only for me but for Bob.

Patti-Jo, you have been in my life for as long as I can remember and I can't thank you enough for everything you have done.

To Caroline, Tina, Maria and Deb. You each in your own ways made me laugh and made me feel cared for.

To Sue and Jack, Vick and Marg, for their entertaining stories and never-ending support.

To the rest of my family and friends, thank you for your kind words, cards, gifts and phone calls. I am so very grateful.

Lastly, to my amazing editor, Jena. This book would not be what it is without your brilliance and patience.

KAREN DAVIDSON ZACHARY LIVES IN Sault Ste. Marie, Ontario, where she worked for thirty years as a customs inspector at the international bridge between Canada and the United States—more specifically on the Canadian side, not in between countries.

Married to her very lucky husband, Bob, Zachary has one amazing son, and she is the "wicked stepmother" to three wonderful stepchildren who have graciously bestowed upon her six spectacular grandchildren. She has a very lazy golden retriever, Molly, and her kindred spirit, the Bernedoodle, Theo.

Karen's adventures have taken her to Florida in a WWII training plane, to Africa to work with women with AIDS, and trips with her girlfriends to Tennessee on her beloved Harley-Davidson Softail. Driving "Tail of the Dragon" is one of her greatest accomplishments.

Made in the USA
Middletown, DE
30 June 2016